THE LIBRARY OF
ROMANTIC
MUSIC

EDITED BY SAM LUNG.
MUSIC COMPILED AND PROCESSED BY CAMDEN MUSIC SERVICES.

THIS BOOK COPYRIGHT © 2015 BY AMSCO PUBLICATIONS,
A DIVISION OF MUSIC SALES CORPORATION, NEW YORK

ORDER NO. AM1006984

EXCLUSIVE DISTRIBUTORS:
MUSIC SALES LIMITED
14–15 BERNERS STREET, LONDON W1T 3LJ, UK.
MUSIC SALES CORPORATION
180 MADISON AVENUE, 24TH FLOOR, NEW YORK NY 10016, USA.
MUSIC SALES PTY. LIMITED
UNITS 3-4, 17 WILLFOX STREET, CONDELL PARK NSW 2200, AUSTRALIA.

PRINTED IN CHINA.

AMSCO PUBLICATIONS
PART OF THE MUSIC SALES GROUP
LONDON/NEW YORK/PARIS/SYDNEY/COPENHAGEN/BERLIN/MADRID/HONG KONG/TOKYO

Contents

Pas De Deux

from Giselle

Adolphe Adam

Mallorca, Op.202

Barcarola

Isaac Albéniz

March To The Scaffold

from Symphonie Fantastique

Hector Berlioz

Allegretto non troppo

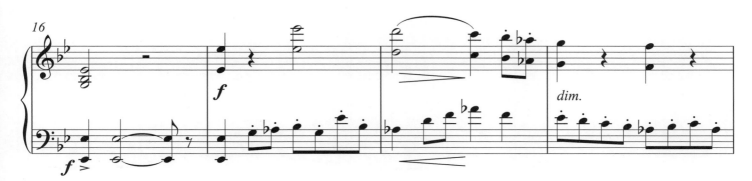

Casta Diva

from Norma

Vincenzo Bellini

Habañera

from Carmen

Georges Bizet

Duet from 'The Pearl Fishers'

Georges Bizet

Prelude

from L'Arlésienne

Georges Bizet

Tempo I

Nocturne

from String Quartet No. 2

Alexander Borodin

Capriccio in G Minor

Op.116 No.3

Johannes Brahms

Hungarian Dance in G Minor

Johannes Brahms

Intermezzo in A Major

Op.118 No.2

Johannes Brahms

Rhapsody No.2 in G Minor

Op.79 No.2

Johannes Brahms

Wiegenlied (Cradle Song)

Op.49 No.4

Johannes Brahms

dim. e rall. al fine

Violin Concerto No.1, Op.26

2nd Movement

Max Bruch

Locus Iste

Anton Bruckner

Cantabile in B♭ Major

Frédéric Chopin

Mazurka in C Major

Op. 7 No. 5

Frédéric Chopin

Mazurka in A Minor

Op.68 No.2

Frédéric Chopin

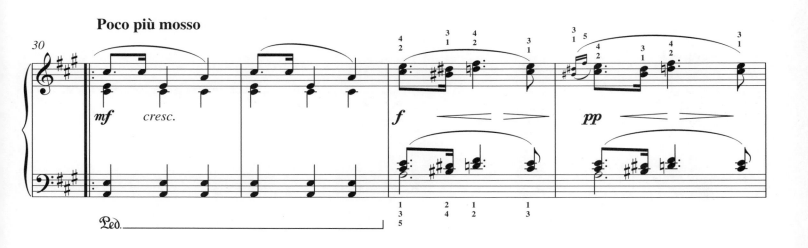

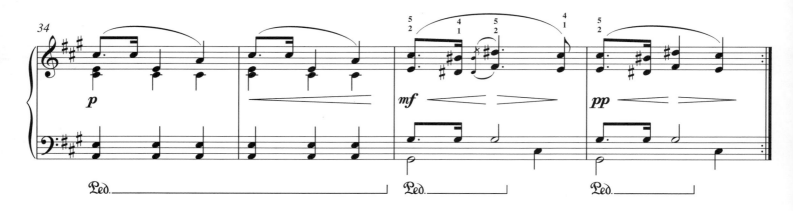

poco a poco rit.

Tempo I

Mazurka in F Major

Op.68 No.3

Frédéric Chopin

Allegretto, ma non troppo

Nocturne in G Minor

Op. 15 No. 3

Frédéric Chopin

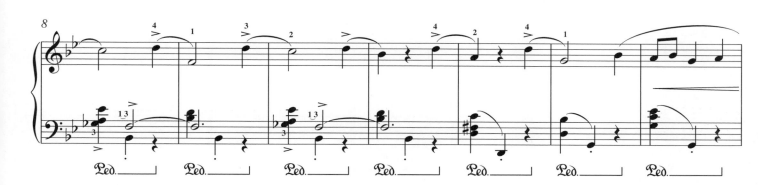

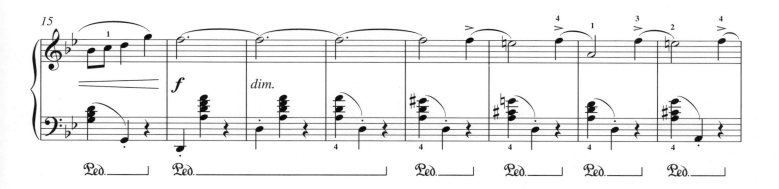

accel.

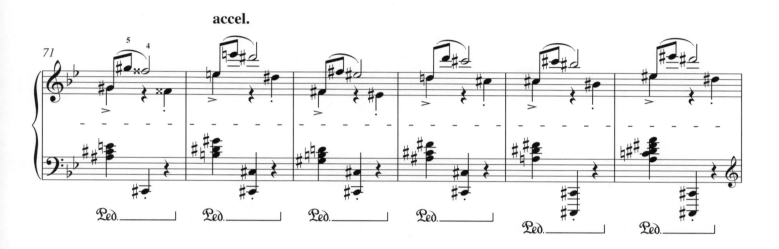

rit.   rall.

a tempo

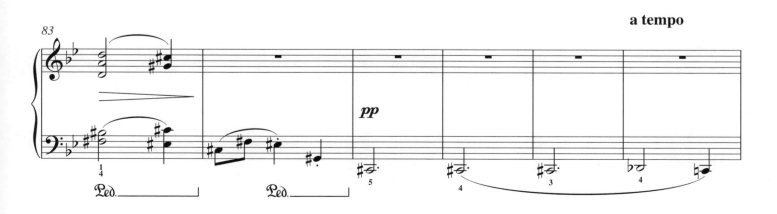

Religioso

sempre legato (con ped.)

Nocturne in E♭ Major

Op.9 No.2

Frédéric Chopin

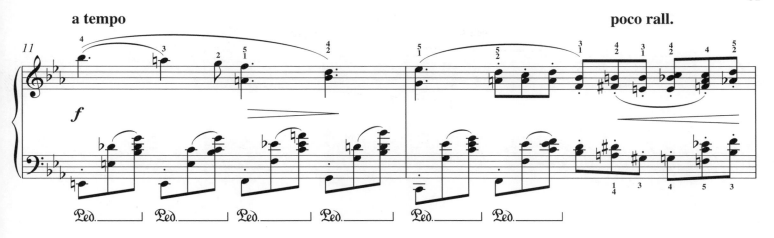

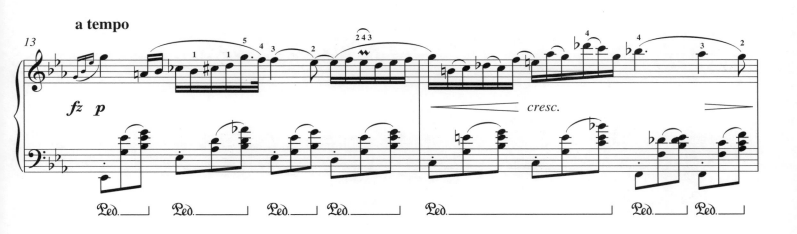

poco rall.   a tempo

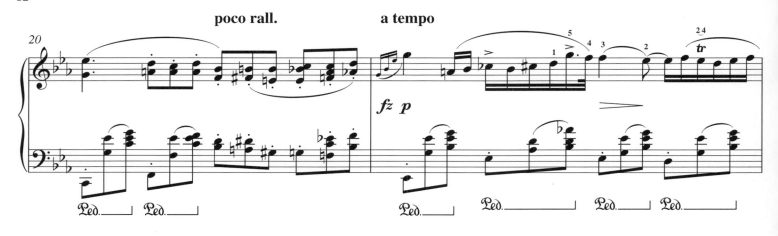

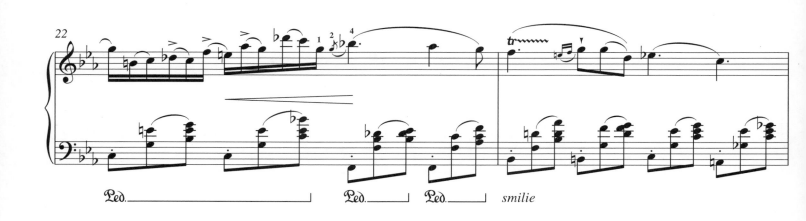

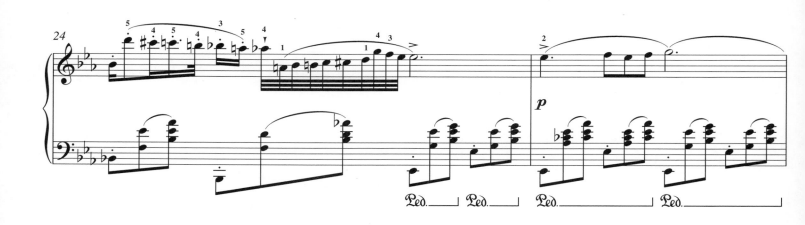

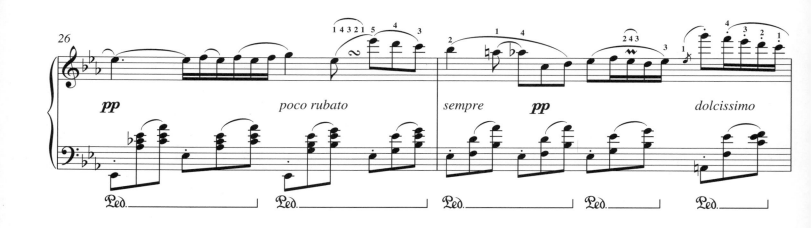

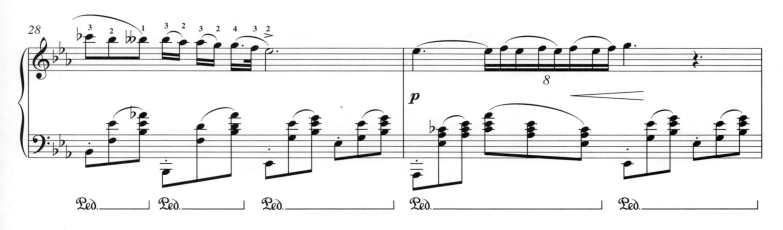

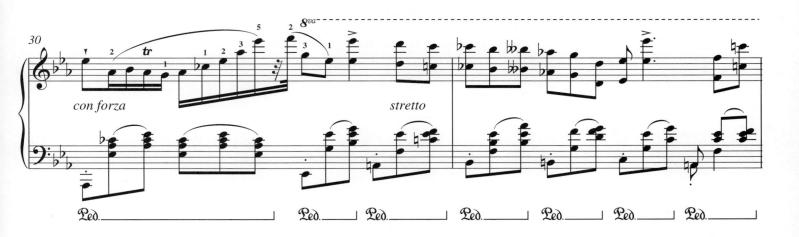

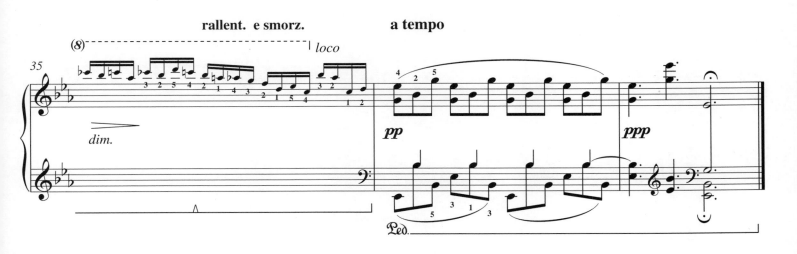

Prelude in E Minor

Op. 28 No. 4

Frédéric Chopin

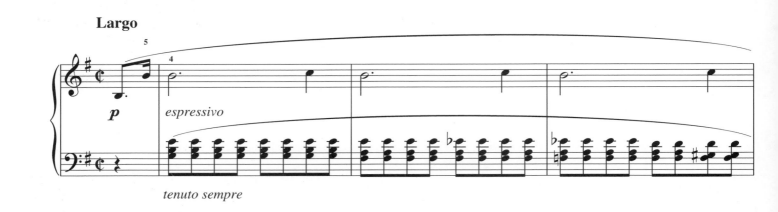

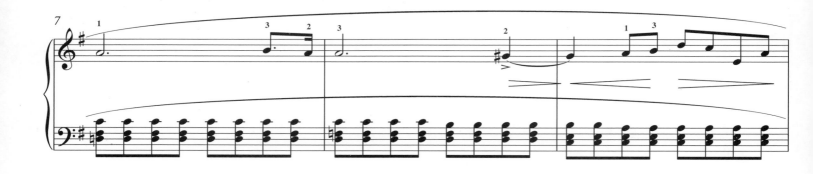

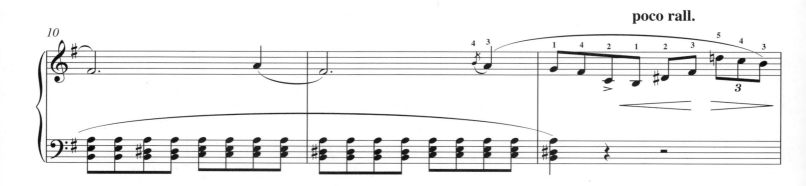

a tempo

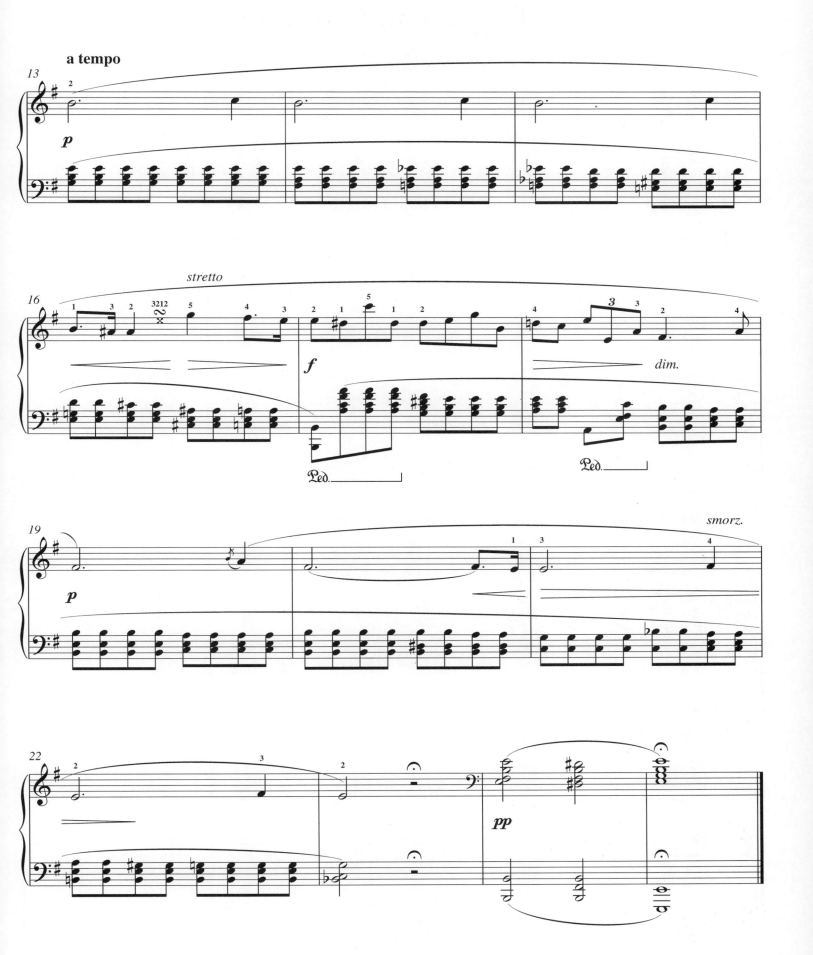

Prelude in E Major

Op. 28 No. 7

Frédéric Chopin

Prelude in C Minor

Op. 28 No. 20

Frédéric Chopin

Romance

2nd Movement *from* Piano Concerto No.1 in E Minor, Op.11

Frédéric Chopin

Waltz in D♭ Major

Op.64 No.1 'Minute Waltz'

Frédéric Chopin

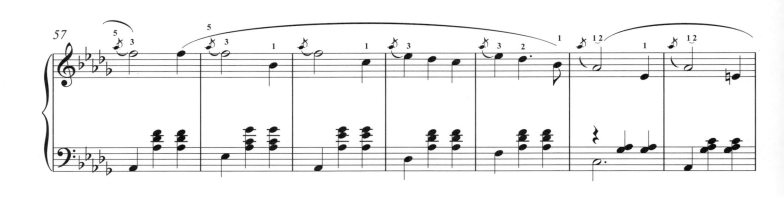

poco rit.

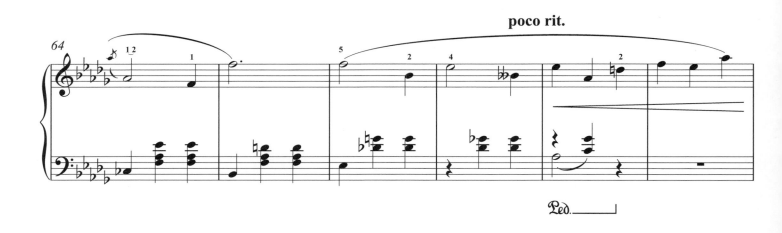

a tempo

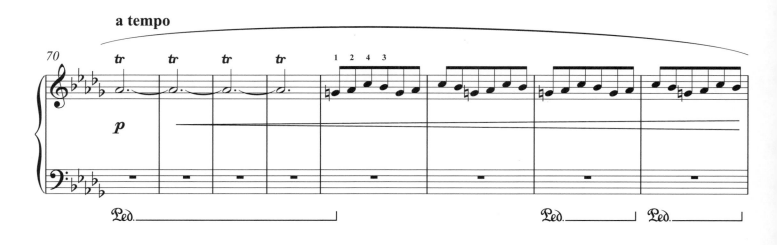

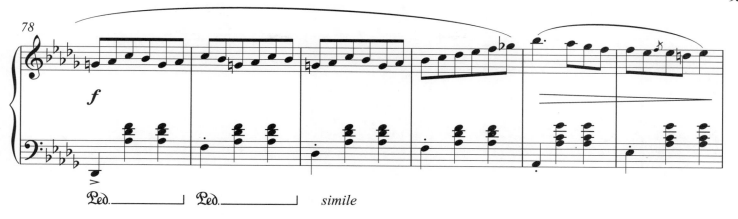

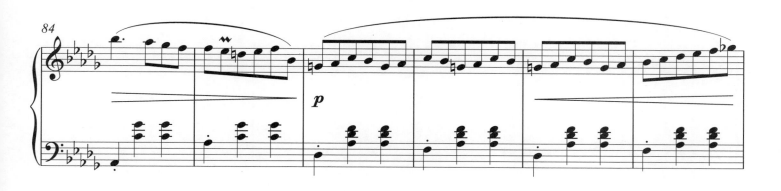

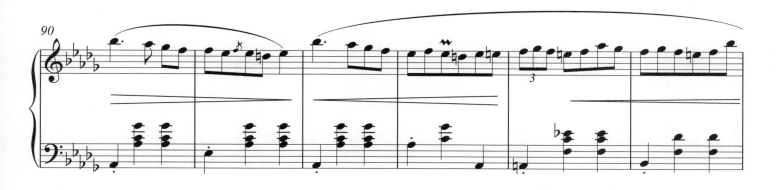

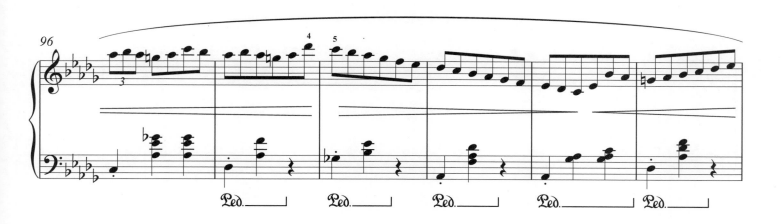

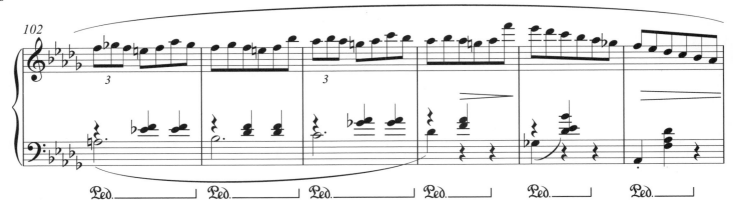

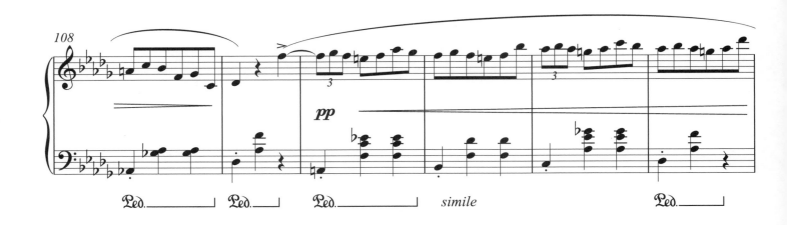

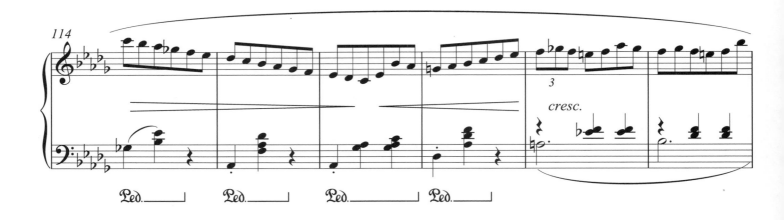

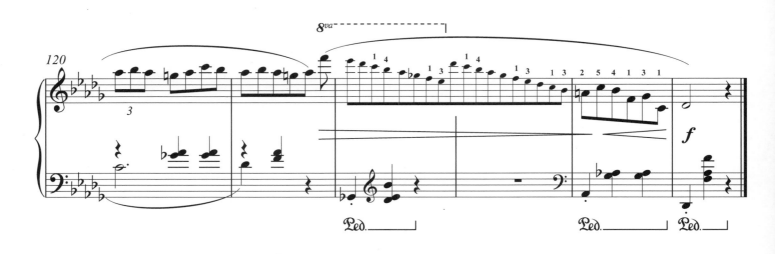

Waltz in A♭ Major

Op.69 No.1 'The Farewell Waltz'

Frédéric Chopin

Demande Et Réponse

from Petite Suite de Concert, Op.77

Samuel Coleridge-Taylor

Serenade For Strings in E Minor

1st Movement

Antonín Dvořák

Solemn Melody

Henry Walford Davies

Clair De Lune

from Suite Bergamasque

Claude Debussy

Andante très expressif

Tempo rubato

Calmato

Tempo I

pp *morendo jusqu'à la fin*

La Cathédrale Engloutie (The Sunken Cathedral)

No.10 *from* Préludes Book 1

Claude Debussy

Profondément calme (dans une brume doucement sonore)

peu à peu sorrant de la brume

augmentez progressivement (sans presser)

sonore sans dureté

Un peu moins lent (Dans une expression allant grandissant)

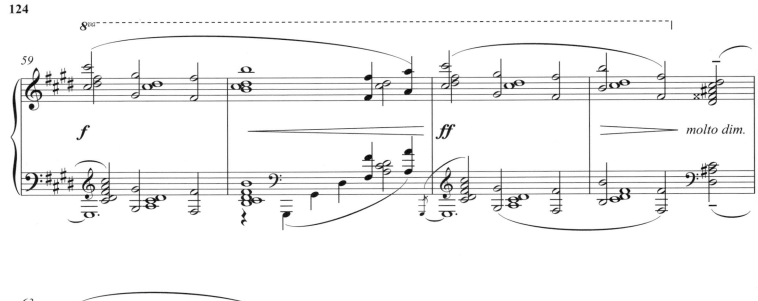

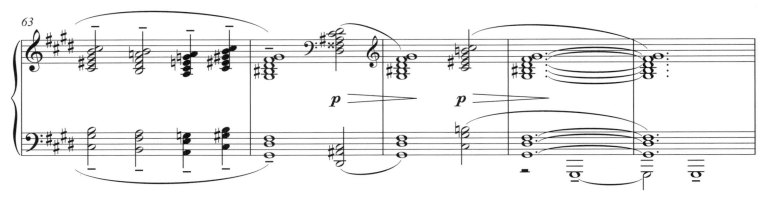

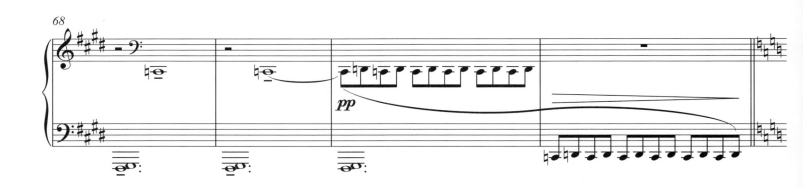

au mouvement

*pp Comme un écho de la phrase
entendue précédemment**

Flottant et sourd

* As an echo of the previous phrase

Valse Romantique

Claude Debussy

Flower Duet

from Lakmé

Léo Delibes

Waltz

from Coppélia

Léo Delibes

Chanson De Matin

Edward Elgar

Land Of Hope And Glory

Pomp And Circumstance March No.1

Edward Elgar

Nimrod

from Enigma Variations, Op. 36

Edward Elgar

Salut D'Amour

Edward Elgar

Agnus Dei

from Requiem

Gabriel Fauré

Après Un Rêve

Gabriel Fauré

Pavane

Gabriel Fauré

Panis Angelicus

César Franck

164

Norwegian Dance

Op. 35 No. 2

Edvard Grieg

Notturno

No.4 *from* Lyric Pieces, Op.54

Edvard Grieg

Ave Maria

Charles Gounod

Danza Lenta

Op. 37 No. 1

Enrique Granados

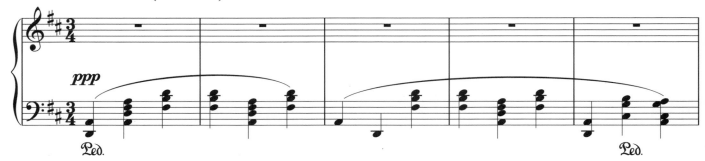

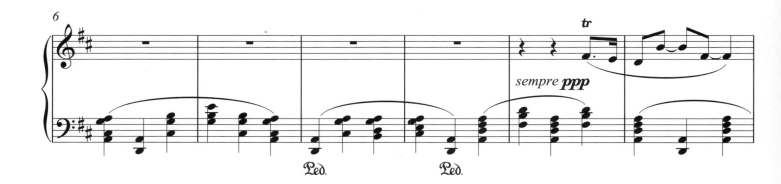

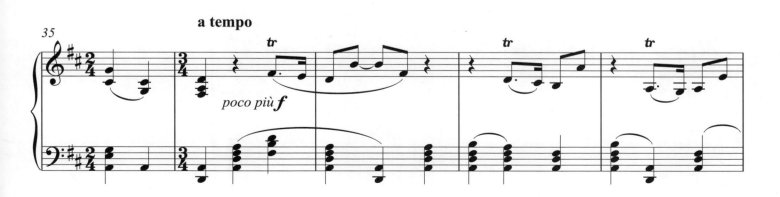

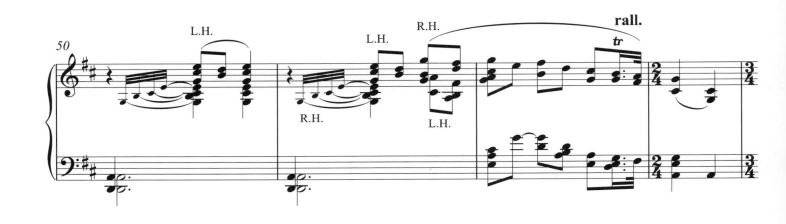

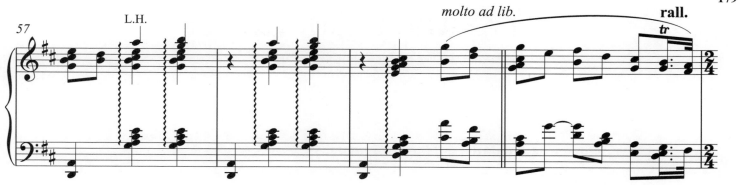

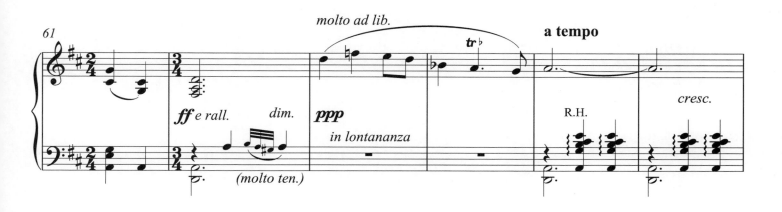

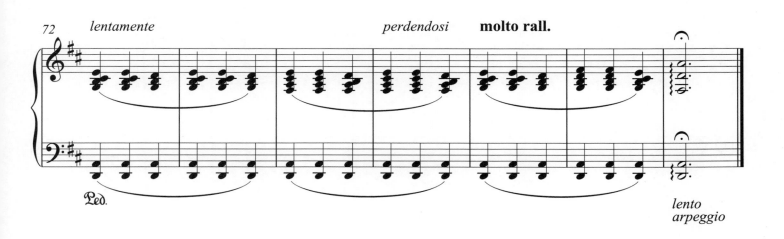

At An Old Trysting-Place

from Woodland Sketches, Op.51

Edward MacDowell

Somewhat quaintly, not too sentimentally

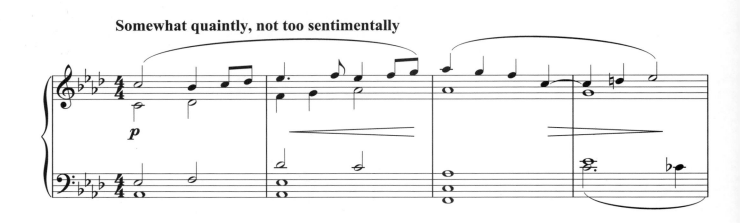

slightly ritard.

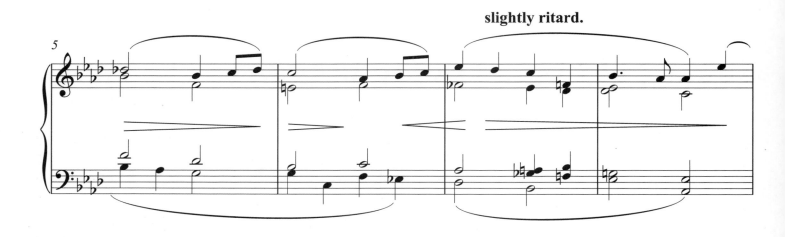

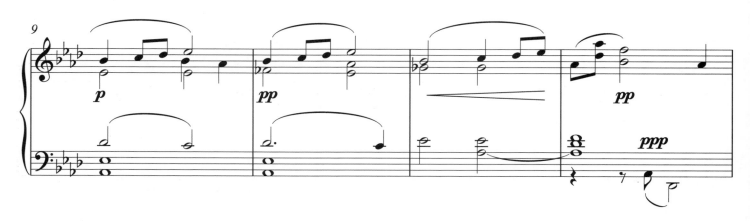

Symphony No.5

4th Movement: Adagietto

Gustav Mahler

Meditation

from Thaïs

Jules Massenet

Rákóczy March

Franz Liszt

Allegro deciso ed energico assai

Cantique d'Amour

Franz Liszt

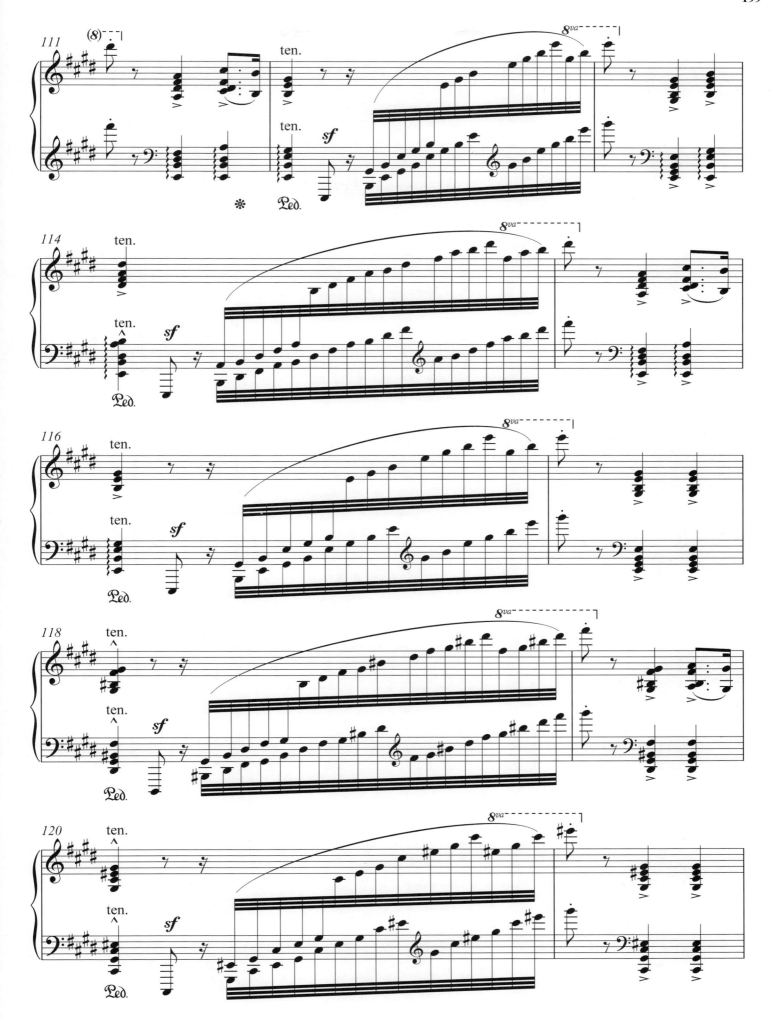

O For The Wings Of A Dove

Felix Mendelssohn

Duetto

Song Without Words, Op. 38 No. 6

Felix Mendelssohn

Sweet Remembrance

Song Without Words, Op. 19b No. 1

Felix Mendelssohn

Gopak

from Sorochinsky Fair

Modest Mussorgsky

Allegretto scherzando

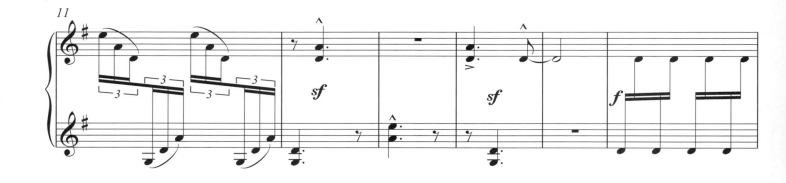

Promenade

from Pictures At An Exhibition

Modest Mussorgsky

Allegro giusto, nel modo russico, senza allegrezza, ma poco sostenuto

Jerusalem

Hubert Parry

Un Bel Di Vedremo

from Madame Butterfly

Giacomo Puccini

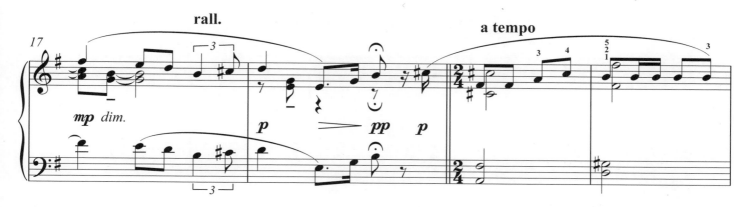

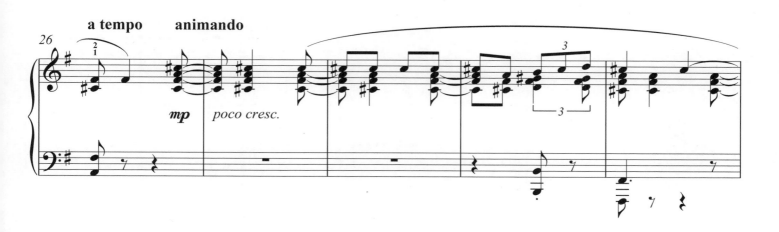

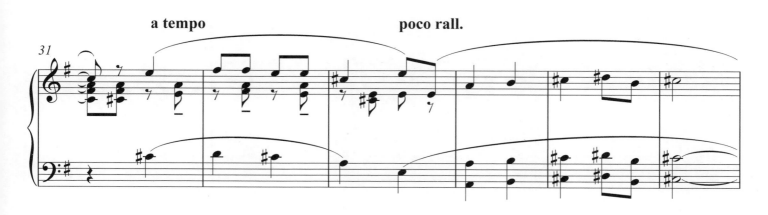

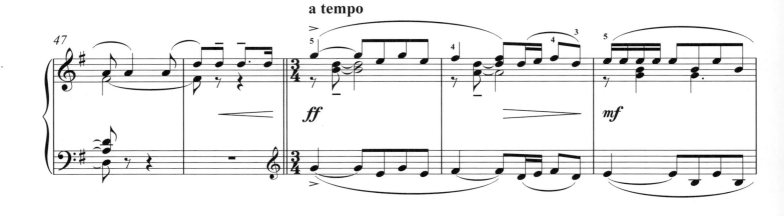

Nessun Dorma

from Turandot

Giacomo Puccini

Vissi d'Arte

from Tosca

Giacomo Puccini

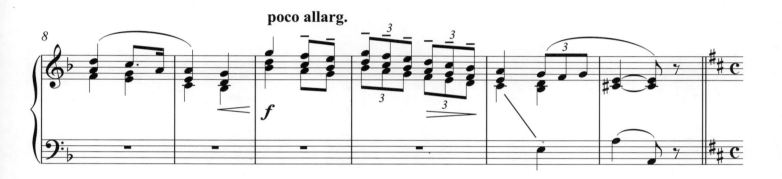

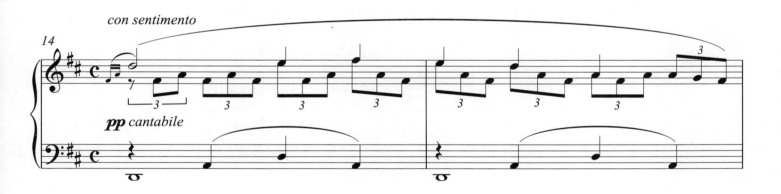

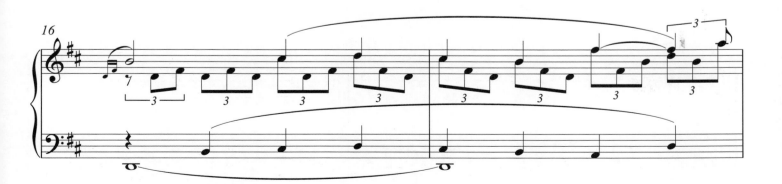

229

The Young Prince And The Young Princess

from Scheherazade

Nikolai Rimsky-Korsakov

Prélude

from Le Tombeau De Couperin

Maurice Ravel

À La Manière De ... Alexander Borodine

Valse

Maurice Ravel

Pavane Pour Une Infante Défunte

Maurice Ravel

1er Mouvt. **Très lointain**

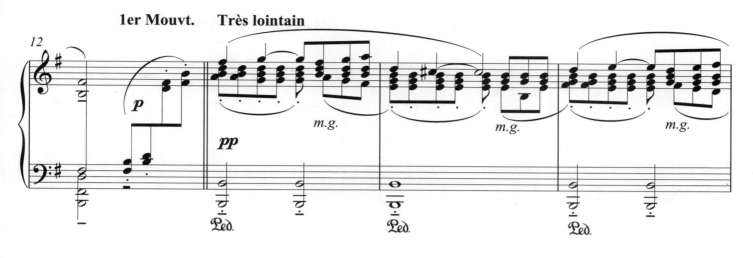

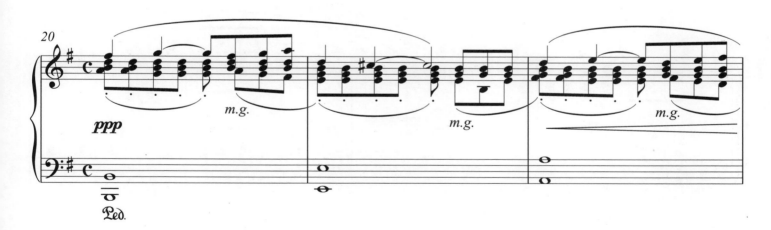

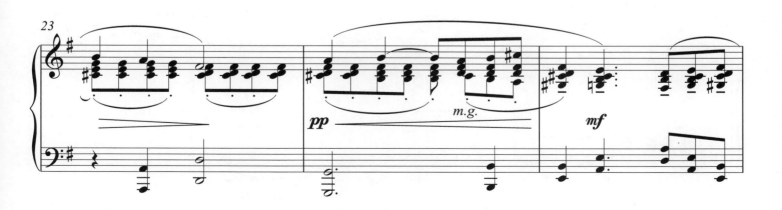

248

Prélude

Maurice Ravel

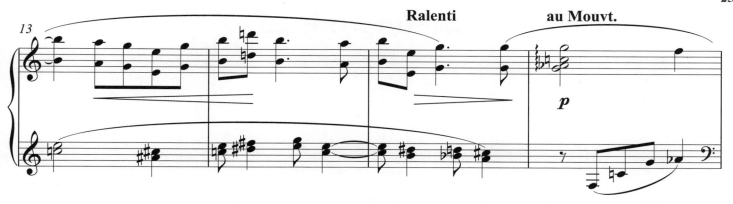

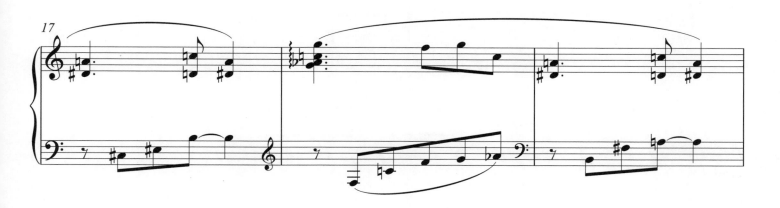

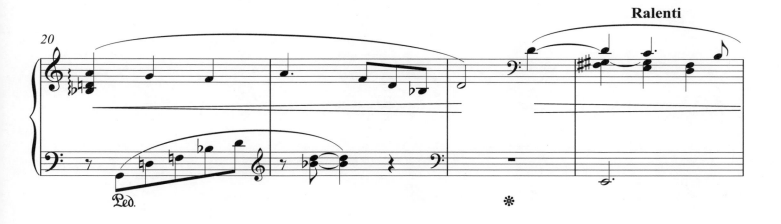

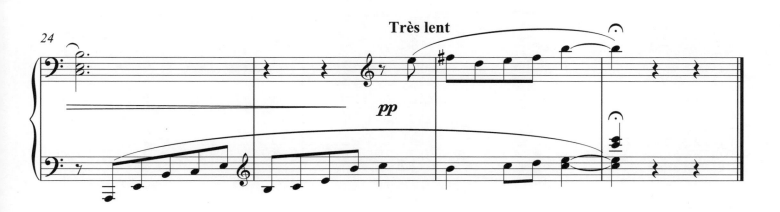

Sonatine

2nd Movement

Maurice Ravel

Softly Awakes My Heart

from Samson And Delilah

Camille Saint-Saëns

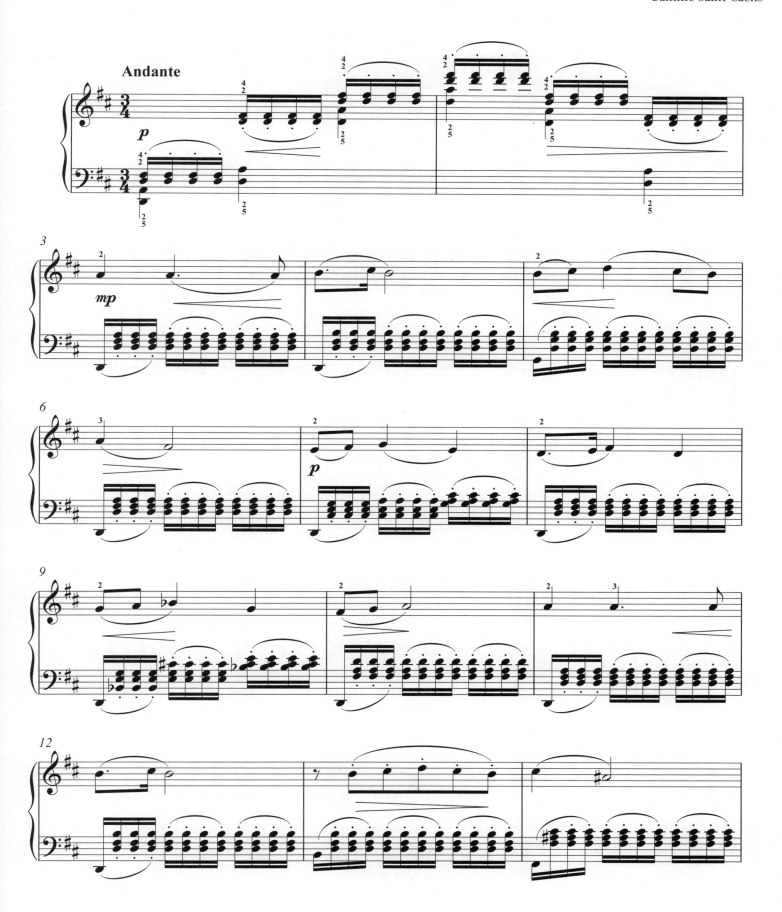

Danse Macabre, Op.40

Camille Saint-Saëns

Mouvement modéré de Valse

Valse-Ballet

Erik Satie

Gute Nacht

from Winterreise, Op.89

Franz Schubert

Impromptu No.3 in G♭ Major

from Four Impromptus, Op.90

Franz Schubert

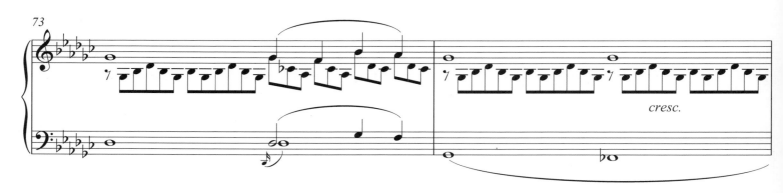

Scherzo

D.593 No.1

Franz Schubert

Chiarina

from Carnaval, Op.9

Robert Schumann

Eintritt

from Waldszenen, Op.82

Robert Schumann

Piano Quartet in E♭ Major, Op.47

3rd Movement

Robert Schumann

cantabile e poco a poco cresc.

rit.

p

The Wild Horseman

from Album For The Young, Op.68

Robert Schumann

Piano Sonata No.2 in G Minor, Op.22

2nd Movement

Robert Schumann

Prelude

Op.11 No.4

Alexander Scriabin

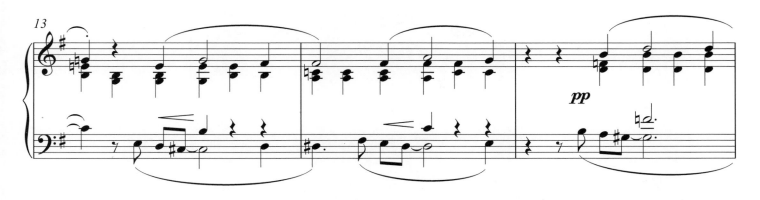

Etude

Op. 2 No. 1

Alexander Scriabin

Radetsky March

Johann Strauss I

Emperor Waltz

Johann Strauss II

Voices Of Spring

Johann Strauss II

June: Barcarolle

No.6 *from* The Seasons, Op.37

Pyotr Ilyich Tchaikovsky

Love Theme

from Romeo And Juliet

Pyotr Ilyich Tchaikovsky

Chinese Dance

from The Nutcracker

Pyotr Ilyich Tchaikovsky

Swan Lake

Act II Finale

Pyotr Ilyich Tchaikovsky

Sweet Reverie

from Album For The Young, Op. 39

Pyotr Ilyich Tchaikovsky

Dies Irae

from Requiem

Giuseppe Verdi

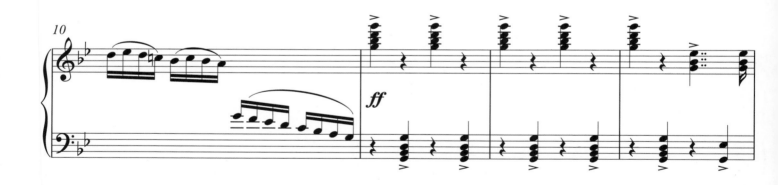

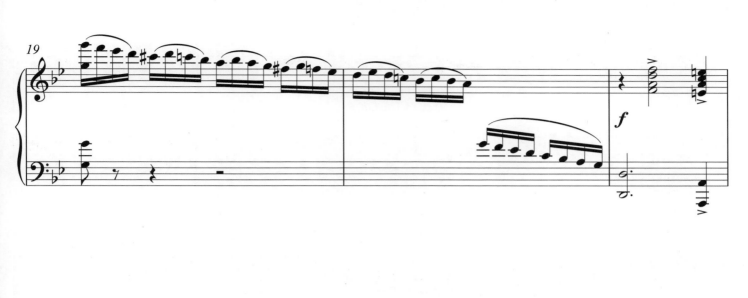

334

Grand March

from Aida

Giuseppe Verdi

Tempo di marcia

Va Pensiero (Chorus Of The Hebrew Slaves)

from Nabucco

Giuseppe Verdi

Cantabile (poco meno mosso)

The Ride Of The Valkyries

from Die Walküre

Richard Wagner

To The Evening Star

from Tannhäuser

Richard Wagner

Andante sostenuto

Sailor's Chorus

from Der Fliegende Holländer (The Flying Dutchman)

Richard Wagner